D1164942

JAN 09

CITIES

NEW YORK CITY

ABDO
Publishing Company

Joanne Mattern

visit us at
www.abdopublishing.com

Published by ABDO Publishing Company, 4940 Viking Drive, Edina, Minnesota 55435.
Copyright © 2007 by Abdo Consulting Group, Inc. International copyrights reserved in all
countries. No part of this book may be reproduced in any form without written permission from
the publisher. The Checkerboard Library™ is a trademark and logo of ABDO Publishing
Company.

Printed in the United States.

Cover Photo: Corbis
Interior Photos: Corbis pp. 1, 5, 6-7, 11, 13, 14, 15, 17, 18, 19, 20, 22, 23, 24, 25, 26, 27, 28, 29;
  North Wind p. 9

Series Coordinator: Megan Murphy
Editors: Heidi M. Dahmes, Megan Murphy
Art Direction & Maps: Neil Klinepier

All U.S. population statistics are from the 2000 census taken by the U.S. Census Bureau.

Library of Congress Cataloging-in-Publication Data

Mattern, Joanne, 1963-
    New York City / Joanne Mattern.
       p. cm. -- (Cities)
    Includes index.
    ISBN-10 1-59679-719-3
    ISBN-13 978-1-59679-719-2
       1. New York (N.Y.)--Juvenile literature. I. Title. II. Series.

 F128.33.M38 2006
 974.7'1--dc22

                                                          2005028753

CONTENTS

NEW YORK CITY

New York City has been an important city for hundreds of years. It was one of the first settlements in the United States. And, it became the nation's first capital.

New York City is in New York State. Today, it is the largest city in the United States. More than 8 million people call the city home. People come from all over the world to live and work there. Most of the city is located on islands. These islands are linked by bridges, tunnels, and ferries.

New York City has faced many difficulties throughout its history. One terrible event occurred on September 11, 2001. That day, a **terrorist** attack destroyed a New York City landmark. It also took the lives of many New Yorkers.

Despite these hardships, New York City has grown to become a center of business, arts, and politics. It is considered one of the world's greatest cities.

New York City lost the World Trade Center towers in the September 11 attack. However, New York still has one of the most distinctive skylines of any U.S. city. From March 11 to April 13, 2002, the Tribute in Lights shone as a memorial to the fallen Twin Towers.

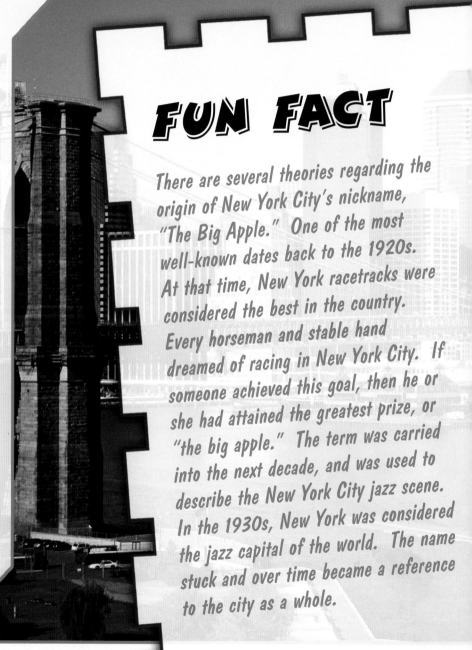

NEW YORK CITY AT A GLANCE

Date of Founding: 1624

Population: 8,008,278

Metro Area: 309 square miles (800 sq km)

Average Temperatures:
- 31° Fahrenheit (-1°C) in cold season
- 72° Fahrenheit (22°C) in warm season

Annual Rainfall: 44 inches (112 cm)

Elevation: 55 feet (17 m)

Landmarks: Statue of Liberty, Empire State Building, Ellis Island

Money: U.S. dollar

Language: English

FUN FACT

There are several theories regarding the origin of New York City's nickname, "The Big Apple." One of the most well-known dates back to the 1920s. At that time, New York racetracks were considered the best in the country. Every horseman and stable hand dreamed of racing in New York City. If someone achieved this goal, then he or she had attained the greatest prize, or "the big apple." The term was carried into the next decade, and was used to describe the New York City jazz scene. In the 1930s, New York was considered the jazz capital of the world. The name stuck and over time became a reference to the city as a whole.

TIMELINE

1524 - The first European arrives on Manhattan Island.

1609 - Henry Hudson claims the Hudson River valley for the Dutch.

1624 - The Dutch settlement of New Amsterdam is founded.

1664 - The British take over Dutch settlements in North America; New Amsterdam is renamed New York.

1789 - New York becomes the first capital of the United States of America. In 1800, the capital moves to Washington, D.C.

1825 - The Erie Canal opens.

1840s - Immigrants begin to arrive in New York Harbor.

1898 - Manhattan unites with the four surrounding boroughs.

1904 - New York City's subway opens.

1964 - Race riots occur in several of New York City's African-American communities.

2001 - On September 11, the World Trade Center towers are destroyed in a terrorist attack.

DUTCH COLONY

People have lived in the New York City area for hundreds of years. Before 1500, Algonquian-speaking tribes lived on present-day Manhattan Island. Then in 1524, the first European arrived. He was an Italian named Giovanni da Verrazano. He was exploring for France.

In 1609, another explorer sailed into New York Harbor. Henry Hudson was an Englishman working for the Dutch. He was looking for a shorter trade route between Europe and Asia.

Hudson did not find the trade route. However, he did claim the entire Hudson River valley for the Dutch. And, his explorations led to the establishment of the Dutch colony of New Netherland. The colony was made up of the present-day states of Connecticut, Delaware, New Jersey, New York, and Pennsylvania.

In 1624, the Dutch West India Company founded a settlement on Manhattan Island. They called it New Amsterdam. However, Native Americans still lived on the

Opposite Page: *In 1609, Henry Hudson sailed his ship, the* Half Moon, *into New York Harbor and up the river that would later bear his name.*

island. So in 1626, the Dutch bought Manhattan Island from the Native Americans. They paid $24 worth of goods for the land.

The British also had colonies in North America around this time. They wanted control of New Amsterdam, too. So in 1664, the British took over the settlement. And, they changed the name to New York to honor James, Duke of York.

BRITISH COLONY

The British ruled the American colonies for more than 100 years. Eventually, the colonists decided they wanted to govern themselves. So, they fought for freedom in the **American Revolution**. In 1783, they won. New York was named the first capital of the United States in 1789. In 1800, Washington, D.C., became the nation's permanent capital.

Still, New York remained important to the new nation. In 1825, the Erie Canal opened. It connected New York State to the Great Lakes. As a result, shipping became a major industry. Soon, New York Harbor was the busiest port in the United States.

New York grew rapidly. During the 1840s, large numbers of **immigrants** began to arrive in the United States. Most entered the country through New York Harbor. Many immigrants made their homes in New York.

Until 1898, New York consisted solely of Manhattan Island. But that year, the surrounding **boroughs** of Brooklyn, Staten Island, the Bronx, and Queens united with Manhattan to form New York City. With a population close to 3 million, it became America's largest city!

Today, the immigration processing center on Ellis Island is a museum.

LAND OF LIBERTY

The U.S. government built a station to process the immigrants who came into the country. This station was on Ellis Island in New York Harbor. Between 1892 and 1954, about 17 million immigrants came through Ellis Island. Four million of those immigrants stayed in New York City.

The Statue of Liberty is located on Liberty Island in New York Harbor. This national monument was a gift of friendship from France to the United States in 1886. The statue came to symbolize freedom and democracy for all the immigrants who passed through the harbor on their way to a better life. In 1965, Ellis Island became part of the Statue of Liberty National Monument.

CITY TROUBLES

During the early 1900s, New York experienced a time of **economic** prosperity. But in 1929, the **stock market** crashed, and the entire country entered the **Great Depression**. About one-quarter of New York City's workforce was unemployed. Then in 1934, Mayor Fiorello La Guardia helped improve economic conditions in the city.

However, problems continued to plague the city. In 1964, racial tension caused violence in several African-American communities. By 1975, New York City was in deep financial trouble. When Rudy Giuliani became mayor in 1994, crime was at an all-time high. Mayor Giuliani instituted several public improvement projects. Conditions started to improve.

Then on September 11, 2001, **terrorists** flew two planes into the World Trade Center. Its twin towers were destroyed, and more than 2,800 people were killed. It was a terrible day for New York City and the United States. Today, the Freedom Tower is being built on the site of the World Trade Center. It will honor the people who died during that tragic event.

The special steel facing on the Chrysler Building's seven-story pinnacle gives the skyscraper its distinctive look.

SKYSCRAPERS

New York City kept on growing during the 1900s. And the buildings in the city became bigger, too.

1902

The Flatiron Building was the first skyscraper in New York City. It is 21 stories tall and is shaped like a skinny triangle!

1930

The Chrysler Building became the tallest building in the world. It is 77 stories tall.

1931

At 102 stories tall, the Empire State Building surpassed the Chrysler Building.

1972

The World Trade Center became the tallest building in New York City. The building's twin towers were 110 stories tall. They soared more than 1,360 feet (415 m) above the ground.

2001

Following the September 11 attack, the Empire State Building was again the tallest building in New York City. However, there are many taller buildings in the world. The Taipei Tower in Taiwan is 1,670 feet (509 m) tall!

CITY HALL

New York City Hall

 Through good and bad times, New York City is led by a mayor. New Yorkers elect their mayor to serve a four-year term. Michael Bloomberg was elected New York City mayor in 2002. His office is in City Hall, which is located in downtown New York.

 New York City is divided into five **boroughs**. They are Manhattan, Brooklyn, the Bronx, Queens, and Staten Island. Each borough elects a president to represent its citizens in the

Because New York is such an important city, the United Nations (UN) established its headquarters there in 1946. UN members work together for world peace.

city government. The mayor and the **borough** presidents work together to ensure that all New Yorkers are treated equally.

The New York City Council also works to help New York's people. The council is the legislative branch of the city government. It has 51 members, and each council member serves a four-year term.

AROUND NYC

Finding your way around Manhattan is easy. Most of the streets and avenues are numbered and laid out in a grid. But other parts of the city, such as the outer **boroughs**, do not follow the grid system. Lower Manhattan can also be confusing. This is the oldest part of New York City. Many of the streets there are winding and narrow.

New York's streets are also very crowded. To get around the city, most New Yorkers use public transportation. This includes buses, trains, and the subway. The city's subway opened in 1904. On average, more than 3 million people use it every day.

New York City is surrounded by water. So, boats called ferries are another popular transportation option. The Staten Island Ferry takes people between Staten Island and Manhattan. Ferries also run between Manhattan and the other boroughs, as well as to New Jersey.

Opposite Page: *Many New Yorkers don't own cars because they can walk or take the subway everywhere they want to go. This way, they also avoid the city's daily traffic jams.*

New York City has two major airports. Both airports are located in Queens. They are named after famous Americans. One airport is named after President John F. Kennedy. The other is called La Guardia Airport. It is named after Fiorello La Guardia. He was New York City's mayor from 1934 to 1945.

BIG BUSINESS

New York City is the nucleus of the U.S. **economy**. About 2,500 major U.S. corporations are located in the city. Many foreign companies have their headquarters in New York as well.

Clothing is New York City's main industry. The Garment District in midtown Manhattan is the city's fashion center. This is the place where the clothing is designed and sold. However, most of the garment factories are located in Brooklyn, Queens, and the Bronx. So, trucks bring clothing in from the suburbs every day of the week.

Shipping is another important industry in New York. New York City is located on the Atlantic Ocean. It also has access to the Great Lakes by way of the Erie Canal. So, the city is a major

Tourism is another important part of New York City's economy. Every year, thousands of people visit the city to see its famous places. Taking care of these tourists creates many jobs. Souvenir shops especially are big moneymakers.

The trading floor of the New York Stock Exchange

seaport. Cargo ships unload foreign products in New York Harbor. Many more goods are brought into the city by air.

New York City is a major financial center, too. Many banks and other financial businesses are found there. Most of the city's business is centered on Wall Street. This financial district is home to the New York Stock Exchange (NYSE). NYSE is the oldest and largest exchange in the U.S. **stock market**.

The city is also a hot spot for book and newspaper publishing. Some of the nation's television studios, radio networks, and advertising agencies are headquartered in New York City as well.

New York City's sidewalks are especially crowded in spring and fall. At these times, people take advantage of the mild weather.

New York City is located where the Hudson and East rivers empty into New York Harbor. The city encompasses Manhattan and Staten islands, the western part of Long Island, and a small part of mainland New York State.

Because of its location on the East Coast, New York City has a moderate climate. Rain falls most often in March and August. Spring and fall are very pleasant. Many people spend time outside during these seasons.

New York City summers can be very hot. Often the temperature goes above 90 degrees Fahrenheit (32°C). The air feels wet and sticky most of the time.

New York City gets snow every winter, but the snow rarely stays long. Winter days are usually cold and windy. However, this can still be a beautiful time of year to be outside.

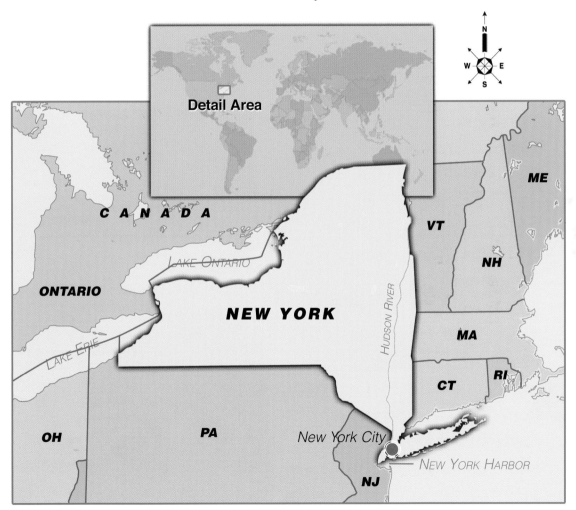

New York City is one of the most **ethnically diverse** cities in the United States. More than 100 years ago, millions of **immigrants** arrived in New York. They came from Italy, Ireland, Poland, Germany, and other European countries. Later, people moved to the city from Latin America.

Today, New York's people come from almost every country in the world. So, New York is filled with ethnic neighborhoods. The Lower East Side is the most famous immigrant neighborhood in the United States. Little Italy and Chinatown are nearby. Many African Americans and

St. Patrick's Cathedral

The Chinese New Year Parade in Chinatown is one of the many ethnic parades in New York City. New York's Chinatown neighborhood has the largest Chinese population outside of Asia.

Hispanics live in the Bronx and upper Manhattan neighborhoods.

The people of New York belong to many different religions. Most New Yorkers are Catholic. St. Patrick's Cathedral is the most prominent Catholic church in the city. The Church of the Transfiguration is near Chinatown. This Catholic church holds several services in Chinese!

The city also has many synagogues, temples, and mosques. These are gathering places for the city's Jews, **Buddhists**, and **Muslims**. Afro-Caribbean religions are found in New York's Puerto Rican, Cuban, and Haitian neighborhoods. These religions are a combination of African and Catholic beliefs.

On any given day, you can hear many different languages on New York City's streets. But, the most common languages are English and Spanish.

Because of high living costs, more people rent than own their homes in New York. Most people live in apartments. There are many high-rise apartment buildings throughout the city. Other people live in

Brownstones in New York City

brownstones. These houses are attached to each other in rows.

You can get almost any kind of food in New York City. There are

Hot dog vendors can be found on practically every street corner in New York City.

more than 25,000 restaurants in the five **boroughs**. They serve everything from pizza to sushi. Street **vendors** sell sandwiches, hot dogs, pretzels, and nuts. New York is also famous for its bagels.

New York City has many public and private schools. There are also several **prestigious** colleges in New York City. Columbia University and New York University are known all over the country. Another famous college is the Juilliard School. Students go there to study music, dance, or theater.

There is a lot to do in New York City! Many people shop in the hundreds of stores all over the city. Others enjoy Central Park, which is in the middle of Manhattan. People walk, ride bikes, or play ball there. The park is also home to a small zoo.

Many parades are held in New York City. The most famous is the Macy's Thanksgiving Day Parade. This parade is filled with floats, marching bands, and huge balloons. Macy's also hosts a huge fireworks display every Fourth of July.

Giant balloons are the stars of the show in the Macy's Thanksgiving Day Parade.

New York City has many sports teams. It is home to the Mets and Yankees baseball teams. The Knicks play basketball, and the Rangers play hockey for New York. The Giants and the Jets are New York's two professional football teams.

Every fall, thousands of people gather to run the New York City Marathon. People also swim and exercise at Chelsea Piers in Manhattan. And each year, the U.S. Open is played in Queens. It is the most important American tennis tournament.

Central Park covers 843 acres (341 ha) of land in the middle of Manhattan. It was the first man-made public park in the United States.

Two stone lions, named Patience and Fortitude, guard the entrance to the New York Public Library.

New York tourists can visit the city's many famous buildings. These include the Empire State Building and the New York Public Library. Other visitors are interested in religious sites such as St. Patrick's Cathedral, the Cathedral of St. John the Divine, or Trinity Church.

The Bronx Zoo is the largest city zoo in the world. This zoo has animals from all over the globe. Next to the zoo is the New York Botanical Garden. Visitors can see beautiful flowers and trees while walking through the garden.

Manhattan has many theaters. Broadway is New York City's number one tourist attraction. Millions of people come to see Broadway shows every year. Others attend operas,

Every year, Times Square hosts the largest New Year's Eve party in the United States. The first New Year's Eve Ball was dropped there in 1908. In 1945, about 2 million people gathered in Times Square to celebrate the end of World War II.

ballets, or concerts at the Brooklyn Academy of Music, Lincoln Center, or Carnegie Hall.

New York is also a city of museums. There are museums about the city's history and **culture**. The American Museum of Natural History has dinosaurs and other amazing displays. There are many famous art museums, too. These include the Metropolitan Museum of Art and the Museum of Modern Art. These attractions make New York City a popular place to visit.

GLOSSARY

American Revolution - from 1775 to 1783. A war for independence between Britain and its North American colonies. The colonists won and created the United States of America.

borough - a division within a city, most specifically of New York City.

Buddhism - a religion founded in India by Siddhartha Gautama. It teaches that pain and evil are caused by desire. If people have no desire, they will achieve a state of happiness called Nirvana.

culture - the customs, arts, and tools of a nation or people at a certain time.

diverse - composed of several distinct pieces or qualities.

economy - the way a nation uses its money, goods, and natural resources.

ethnic - of or having to do with a group of people who have the same race, nationality, or culture.

Great Depression - the period from 1929 to 1942 of worldwide economic trouble when there was little buying or selling, and many people could not find work.

immigrate - to enter another country to live. A person who immigrates is called an immigrant.

Muslim - a person who follows Islam. Islam is a religion based on the teachings of the prophet Muhammad as they appear in the Koran.

prestigious - highly regarded, known for excellence.

stock market - a place where stocks and bonds, which represent parts of businesses, are bought and sold.

terrorist - a person who uses violence to threaten people or governments.

vendor - a person who sells something.

SAYING IT

borough – BUHR-oh
Fiorello La Guardia – fee-uh-REHL-oh luh GWAHRD-ee-uh
Giovanni da Verrazano – joh-VAHN-nee dah vayr-aht-SAHN-oh
Giuliani – joo-lee-AHN-ee
Juilliard – JOOL-ee-ahrd
mosque – MAHSK
synagogue – SIH-nuh-gahg

WEB SITES

To learn more about New York City, visit ABDO Publishing Company on the World Wide Web at **www.abdopublishing.com**. Web sites about New York City are featured on our Book Links page. These links are routinely monitored and updated to provide the most current information available.

INDEX